THIS BOOK BELONGS TO:

____

____

____

We dedicate this book to
Jackson and Whitman,
the two boys
who give us faith and hope
every single day.
may their inspiration give you strength,
just as it has given the two of us.
We pray you find comfort in these pages.

Amanda and Lindsey

We're so glad you've found your way into the pages of this devotional, and we want you to know right from the start— you are not alone in this journey. We are Amanda and Lindsey, two Ohio moms who are caregivers and fierce advocates. We found out how much we needed each other to navigate parenting children with disabilities, the uphill battle of advocacy, and balancing a world full of unexpected challenges.

Inside these pages, you'll find 52 devotionals consisting of Bible verses, prayers, reflections, room for your thoughts and notes, and devotional check-in pages. In addition, there are letters written by us to you, to God, to ourselves, and to our children.

This book may sit on your bed side stand and be used on your toughest days, you may love the connection and use it to start every morning, or you may commit to opening it up once a week and using it to get you through the next year.....all are completely perfect, and know that we are here no matter what you choose.

We have organized this devotional into four sections:

Walk by Faith: When the road gets tough, it's our faith that keeps us moving forward, believing that there's purpose in every step.

Finding Comfort: These devotionals are about finding moments of peace and knowing that God is with us. We hope this section helps you find the comfort you need, whenever that may be.

Love Conquers All: There's nothing stronger than love. In this section, we celebrate the love that sustains us, the love that never gives up, and the love that sees us through the hardest days.

There's Always Hope: Hope is what lifts our spirits and helps us see the light, even when things feel incredibly difficult to navigate.

We've been praying that you would receive this book. We know that caregiving life is hard, and some days, it feels like you can't come up for air. We've both been there. Those days, weeks, months, and years can seem so defeating, You aren't alone, dear mama. You are not forgotten. God is here. He's in the situations that you don't even know about. Please know we are right here, praying for you.

dear god,

I want to thank you for being so patient with me. Knowing our relationship is not dependent on *when*, but rather *how* I choose to pour myself into leaning into you. Seeking faith in God means it's never the wrong time, and that you're never too late. Thank you for holding space for me in my frustration, fear, and grief over an autism diagnosis. I was so young, exhausted, and overwhelmed that I couldn't see where faith fit in to my life except for something to blame for the changes in "my plans." Thank you for granting me the space I needed, but for never pressing pause on the constant yet subtle invitations to learn along with my faith.

I pray for your guidance through these next years. Your wisdom to navigate the complexities of raising a child with a disability in a sometimes less than kind world. Give me wisdom to see the opportunities to each others about differences, to always lead with kindness, even if it feels unwarranted. Please continue to give me patience--patience with others, patience with myself, and above all else patience with my children. I will need you to remind me to press pause, rush less, and celebrate more. Please remind me to celebrate every small victory with enthusiasm and extreme attention.

Please help me keep him safe, Lord, and let me always be able to show him how cherished he is. I pray you always help our family find the strength to move forward, even when it feels scary. I ask that you continue to place incredible people in our life to help us navigate this unique journey with Jackson. May our love for him and others always always be a testament to the love you have shown all of us.

Please continue to guide us and bless us with your love and grace.

dear god,

I want to apologize first. I know I haven't been the best over the years. The challenges that have happened have made me a little bitter at times. It's taken me a while to say this but thank you for those challenges, for without them, I wouldn't have this life that I'm so grateful for.

Thank you for not turning me into a pillar of salt, like Lot's wife, when I look back and think about things that have been lost. While some of the losses have left huge voids in my life, I know they are all a part of your plan. Thank you for the amazing family that you helped me build.

I know that it's nothing short of a miracle that my kids and I are here together. Please forgive me if I ever take this life for granted. I know that there will be challenges; every life has them, but please know I'm trying my hardest not to be bitter and to accept that this is a part of my story to better your kingdom.

I pray that my words in this book help just one caregiver. You say that you are near to the brokenhearted, and I firmly believe that. Thank you for this "laugh until you cry,
cry until you laugh life.

♡,

lindsey

walk by
faith

walk by faith

"Trust in the Lord
with all your heart,
and do not lean on
your own understanding."
Proverbs 3:5

I know trusting in the Lord can be
so difficult when it feels like there
are no answers to your questions.
"Why?"
"What does the future hold?"
"When will it get easier?"
I know, because I've asked all of
the same questions. I've asked them
out of anger and frustration of things
that didn't make any sense.
Or so I thought.
As soon as I stopped worrying about
how things fit into "My Plan" and
remembered everything is in His plan,
I found my peace, and began to trust again.

DEVOTIONAL CHECK -IN

DATE: _______________________________   S M T W T F S

TODAY I'M GRATEFUL FOR

-
-
-

TODAY'S AFFIRMATION

-
-
-
-

SOMETHING I'M PROUD OF

-
-
-
-

NOTES / REMINDERS

"When I desperately want
to know why,
I remember that
Jesus had
all the answers,
and He still wept."
John 11:35

Crying is often seen as a sign of
weakness, but I'm a firm believer
that it is a sign of strength.
Jesus was the son of God, the
picture of perfection, and the
weight of the world
still made him weep.
So, if today is a day where
you need to cry,
go right ahead, it's ok.

DEVOTIONAL CHECK -IN

DATE: ___________________________   S   M   T   W   T   F   S

TODAY I'M GRATEFUL FOR

-
-
-

TODAY'S AFFIRMATION

- ___________________________
- ___________________________
- ___________________________
- ___________________________

SOMETHING I'M PROUD OF

- ___________________________
- ___________________________
- ___________________________
- ___________________________

NOTES / REMINDERS

"Then I pray to you, O Lord.
I say, 'You are my place of
refuge.
You are all I really want in life.
Hear my cry.
Psalm 142: 5-6

The unknown often leaves me
feeling extremely uncomfortable,
and makes me extremely anxious,
or sometimes fearful. These are
the days where the most important,
and most helpful thing I can do
is surrender.
"God, what do you want me to
know today?"
"What do you want me to see?"
"What do you want me to do?"

And then I sit in the silence, and wait.

DEVOTIONAL CHECK -IN

DATE: ______________________________   S M T W T F S

TODAY I'M GRATEFUL FOR

-
-
-

TODAY'S AFFIRMATION

-
-
-
-

SOMETHING I'M PROUD OF

-
-
-
-

NOTES / REMINDERS

4 walk by faith

”For we walk by faith,
not by sight.”
2 Corinthians 5:7

Father God, please watch over
my steps as I walk with You.
Teach me to walk in all wisdom and truth.
Give me discernment to recognize
paths that lead to destruction,
and grant me power
in Your Spirit to resist
the temptation to follow those paths.
Remain near to me as I walk with You.
In Jesus' name, amen.

FREE THOUGHTS

____

____

____

____

DEVOTIONAL CHECK -IN

DATE: _________________________________   S M T W T F S

TODAY I'M GRATEFUL FOR

-
-
-

TODAY'S AFFIRMATION

-
-
-
-

SOMETHING I'M PROUD OF

-
-
-
-

NOTES / REMINDERS

5 walk by faith

"Therefore encourage one another and build one another up, just as you are doing."
1 Thessalonians 5:11

God is a friend who loves us, and He is
right beside us, even in the quietest
moments of doubt or worry.
The most important gift we can offer
others is a space to feel heard.
In these moments, find a friend, and
ask them to sit with you in the
quiet moments.
Offer them a safe space to share their
fears, hold them up in your daily
prayers.
Listen to them. Sit with them when
they need you. Offer moments of quiet,
if that's what they need.

____

____

____

____

DEVOTIONAL CHECK -IN

DATE: _______________________   S M T W T F S

TODAY I'M GRATEFUL FOR

-
-
-

TODAY'S AFFIRMATION

- _______________________
- _______________________
- _______________________
- _______________________

SOMETHING I'M PROUD OF

- _______________________
- _______________________
- _______________________
- _______________________

NOTES / REMINDERS

"For I know the plans
I have for you."
Jeremiah 29:11

God declared that He had a plan for you, which is insane. On days when everything is falling apart, it's important to remember that we must walk by faith and endure the hard because it's part of God's plan to use you as his vessel. What are you hoping is in God's plan for you?

DEVOTIONAL CHECK -IN

DATE: ___________________________   S   M   T   W   T   F   S

TODAY I'M GRATEFUL FOR

-
-
-

TODAY'S AFFIRMATION

- ___________________________
- ___________________________
- ___________________________
- ___________________________

SOMETHING I'M PROUD OF

- ___________________________
- ___________________________
- ___________________________
- ___________________________

NOTES / REMINDERS

7 walk by faith

> "Stand firm in the faith,
> be courageous; be strong."
> 1 Corinthians 16:13

Sometimes courage looks like
admitting when life feels too heavy
to navigate on your own.
Courage means asking God for help,
and waiting for the whisper.
Consider releasing your struggle
back to God today.
Think about what feels too difficult
to navigate alone at the moment.
Release that to God, ask
Him to walk alongside this season
of life with you to ease your worry.
That's courage. That is strength.

____
____
____
____

DEVOTIONAL CHECK -IN

DATE: _______________________________   S   M   T   W   T   F   S

TODAY I'M GRATEFUL FOR

-
-
-

TODAY'S AFFIRMATION

-
-
-
-

SOMETHING I'M PROUD OF

-
-
-
-

NOTES / REMINDERS

"I know the Lord is always with me. I will not be shaken, for He is right beside me."
Psalm 16:8

We have to keep our focus on God. When we forget the outside world and focus on God, we can't be shaken by the things in this world. When we focus on God, we see all the tiny little miracles that we may have missed worrying about the world around us.
How can you focus more on God?

____

____

____

____

DEVOTIONAL CHECK -IN

DATE: _______________________   S   M   T   W   T   F   S

TODAY I'M GRATEFUL FOR

-
-
-

TODAY'S AFFIRMATION

- _______________________
- _______________________
- _______________________
- _______________________

SOMETHING I'M PROUD OF

- _______________________
- _______________________
- _______________________
- _______________________

NOTES / REMINDERS

"Now faith is the assurance
of things hoped for,
the conviction of
things not seen."
Hebrews 11:1

Faith is simply believing in something real
that we can't yet prove.
The best example is Noah building the
Ark when God told him to.
He didn't fully understand why,
but he did it. He trusted God
with his life, even though he couldn't
comprehend it all.
Like Noah, we need to have faith,
even though we are struggling to
understand God's full plan.

What are some challenges you are facing?

DEVOTIONAL CHECK -IN

DATE: _________________________________   S M T W T F S

TODAY I'M GRATEFUL FOR

-
-
-

TODAY'S AFFIRMATION

-
-
-
-

SOMETHING I'M PROUD OF

-
-
-
-

NOTES / REMINDERS

"Blessed is the man who trusts in the Lord, whose trust is the Lord. He is like a tree planted by water, that sends out its roots by the stream, and does not fear when heat comes, for its leaves remain green, and is not anxious in the year of drought, for it does not cease to bear fruit."
Jeremiah 17:7-8

Bloom where you're planted. Sometimes, it's hard to do, but God calls us to trust him and bloom. It can feel lonely during the process, but God will use your story to help the next family. There's a reason that you were given such precious cargo as a caretaker.

DEVOTIONAL CHECK -IN

DATE: _______________________________   S M T W T F S

TODAY I'M GRATEFUL FOR

-
-
-

TODAY'S AFFIRMATION

-
-
-
-

SOMETHING I'M PROUD OF

-
-
-
-

NOTES / REMINDERS

"Because God has said,
'Never will I leave you,
never will I forsake you.'"
Hebrews 13:5

God, I know you see me getting frustrated,
begging to escape certain parts of my life.
I welcome moments of change.
Change can feel scary, but it often
can be beautiful.
Thank you for being a constant presence
in my life, Lord.
Your steadiness gives me hope in the
middle of life's storms.

"Jesus Christ is the same yesterday,
today, and forever."
Hebrews 13:8

DEVOTIONAL CHECK -IN

DATE: _______________________   S   M   T   W   T   F   S

TODAY I'M GRATEFUL FOR

-
-
-

TODAY'S AFFIRMATION

- _______________
- _______________
- _______________
- _______________

SOMETHING I'M PROUD OF

- _______________
- _______________
- _______________
- _______________

NOTES / REMINDERS

"I could ask the darkness to hide me and the light around me to become night — but even in darkness I cannot hide from you.
To you the night shines as bright as day. Darkness and light are the same to you."
Psalm 139: 11-12

Rejoice always. It seems so difficult to rejoice always because not everything is worth rejoicing. Even on our hardest days, we must find something good because God is good.
What is something you can rejoice about?

____

____

____

____

DEVOTIONAL CHECK -IN

DATE: _______________________________________   S   M   T   W   T   F   S

TODAY I'M GRATEFUL FOR

-
-
-

TODAY'S AFFIRMATION

- ____________________________
- ____________________________
- ____________________________
- ____________________________

SOMETHING I'M PROUD OF

- ____________________________
- ____________________________
- ____________________________
- ____________________________

NOTES / REMINDERS

"God loved us, before we were capable of loving Him, and we can only love others because of what He has done in our lives."
John 4:19

I often wondered if it mattered when I dove back into my faith. Did the years that I was angry with God matter? Were they "counted against me," in a way? What I know now to be true is how we show up in the present, it isn't about keeping score, or comparing the past to the present. It's about making the moments count now.

DEVOTIONAL CHECK -IN

DATE: _________________________________   S M T W T F S

TODAY I'M GRATEFUL FOR

-
-
-

TODAY'S AFFIRMATION

-
-
-
-

SOMETHING I'M PROUD OF

-
-
-
-

NOTES / REMINDERS

Finding Comfort

dear self,

I know that it's hard. You are a new mom and the expectations are so high. I know that you feel the overwhelming guilt because you couldn't carry Whit to term. Just breathe. He will be fine. Things aren't going to remotely go as you have planned and that's ok. I promise you that through the hard, you'll see the beauty in the brokenness. You'll realize that although things aren't textbook and no one understands what you're going through, the loneliness is your superpower.

It'll force you to never want this for anyone else so when you put your advocacy pants on in the future, you're fighting for every mom who has gone before you, and every mom who will be in your spot. Try and enjoy most of it. You'll be told that Whit will be your only baby. You won't grieve it, because you are too far into survival mode to even acknowledge it. He won't be your only baby. You'll have a sweet baby girl who won't snuggle with you and you'll feel like you're failing her because all of Whit's diagnoses will come within a few months of each other.

 Spoiler alert! The baby you will agonize over turns into the sassiest, sweet, fun tiny terrorist that you are exhausted by and can't get enough of. She loves her family hard and protects Whit fiercely. Whitman still doesn't have words. It's ok. He's made so much progress with his communication in the last year that it doesn't matter that he isn't speaking with his mouth.

He's also going to excel at school and find his people. It's a fight in the beginning, but the prayers you have been praying for years, that feel empty, are going to bring you Sarah. She's going to make all of your fears go away. She's going to push inclusion and give Whitman the school life he deserves. You're going to get so many new people to your team that genuinely love Whitman it will feel overwhelming. Whitman will have friends, ones that invite him places and want to have playdates. You'll find your people, the ones that don't disappear when they see your life. The ones that show up on hard days. They'll be an ear to listen, they'll bring a laugh, and maybe a casserole. You'll be so grateful for everyone

He's also going to excel at school and find his people. It's a fight in the beginning, but the prayers you have been praying for years, that feel empty, are going to bring you Sarah. She's going to make all of your fears go away. She's going to push inclusion and give Whitman the school life he deserves. You're going to get so many new people to your team that genuinely love Whitman it will feel overwhelming. Whitman will have friends, ones that invite him places and want to have playdates. You'll find your people, the ones that don't disappear when they see your life. The ones that show up on hard days. They'll be an ear to listen, they'll bring a laugh, and maybe a casserole. You'll be so grateful for everyone.

Marriage is hard. You and Jeremy do an amazing job of balancing. But you'll go through a weird time. It's nothing terrible there isn't a lot of fighting or drama but things are just weird. You're both tired and overwhelmed by the gravity of your future with Whit. And life takes a huge unexpected turn and you're forced on a hard journey by yourself. It's a process. I promise Jeremy will surprise you and exceed your expectations. He has come a long way from the early days of doctors appointments. During your weird time, a pandemic happens and while others are suffering, you and Jeremy find time to figure out all the weird.

 I know that you probably already know this, but don't for a second take any person for granted. Your life is going to change a lot over the years and when you look back, you won't recognize it. That's ok. Be grateful. It's ok to feel weak in moments of hard and grief, and there will be plenty of moments of hard and grief, but over anything be grateful. Hold on tight, because it's a wild ride. Be proud of the person you've become she had a lot of hard nights to become this person. Strive for progress over perfection. Love your people hard and hold sweet Whit a little tighter for he is the reason you are who you are today. You've got this. Know that.

lindsey

dear self,

Please promise me to make the effort to be kinder to yourself. You've spent a lot of years worrying that you weren't doing enough, making the right choices, and questioning every reaction you've had during the hard days. Trust me, when you can go back on more sleep, and less emotion, you'll see that you did your best, and it was wonderful. Your dedication to your loved one, your strength, and your love and care are not going unnoticed.

I know you are terrified about what the future will hold, and worrying about it occupies a lot of your thoughts. Let this be the invitation to set the weight of that down, and truly enjoy where you are right now in the journey. So much of this life gets consumed with worrying about the things we cannot control, I want to remind you to press pause and live more in the moment.

Being a caregiver to a child with a disability has taught me about true strength, resilience, and trust. The strength to never let our story be one without beauty, opportunities, and love beyond measure. The resilience to never give up hope, and to never stop pushing the envelope for inclusion and new supports. Learning to trust that there are good people in this world who believe in my boy just as much as I do, and truly want to see him succeed and live a full and amazing life.

Take the time to look for the lessons in the day to day. There are incredible moments woven into each day that we could have never planned, but those lessons are the one's that change our entire outlook on life. Remember to see the extraordinary in the moments that may feel extremely ordinary. Kindness from one child to another, a new solution to a frustrating problem, seeing the smile of a stranger, when your child tries something new... learn from their lead.

Please know there is a community of caregivers who understand your struggles and truly want to support you. You don't have to do this alone. I know sometimes it feels like you are on this journey alone, but don't allow yourself to stay isolated. You need others who you can share things with. And some of the most impactful advocacy work you will do is bringing caregivers together so they can connect and combat isolation.

Most importantly, you have to take care of yourself too. Take the time to figure out who you are outside of being a caregiver. Define yourself as a friend, keep interests, explore your faith, whatever helps you feel like you, find the time to do more of that, and know that your extreme dedication and love are a gift to this world.

amanda

"Your word is a lamp for my feet,
a light for my path. "
Psalm 119:105

"I will always thank the Lord:
I will never stop praising Him.

I will praise Him for what he has done;
may all who are oppressed listen
and be glad!

Proclaim with me the Lord's greatness;
let us praise His name together!

I prayed to the Lord, and He answered me;
He freed me from all my fears."
A prayer for Thanksgiving
Psalm 34 : 1-4

____

____

____

____

DEVOTIONAL CHECK -IN

DATE: _______________________________   S M T W T F S

TODAY I'M GRATEFUL FOR

-
-
-

TODAY'S AFFIRMATION

- _______________________________
- _______________________________
- _______________________________
- _______________________________

SOMETHING I'M PROUD OF

- _______________________________
- _______________________________
- _______________________________
- _______________________________

NOTES / REMINDERS

15 Finding comfort

"This is the message we have heard from him and declare to you: God is light; in Him there is no darkness at all."
1 John 1:5

"You are the light of the world—
like a city on a hilltop that
cannot be hidden. No one lights
a lamp and then puts it under a
basket. Instead, a lamp is placed
on a stand, giving everyone in
the house light. In the same
way, let your good deeds shine
out for all to see so that everyone
will praise your heavenly
Father." Matthew 5:14-16

How can you be a light?

DEVOTIONAL CHECK -IN

DATE: _________________________   S   M   T   W   T   F   S

TODAY I'M GRATEFUL FOR

-
-
-

TODAY'S AFFIRMATION

-
-
-
-

SOMETHING I'M PROUD OF

-
-
-
-

NOTES / REMINDERS

"But those who hope in the
Lord will renew their
strength. They will soar on
wings like eagles; they will
run and not grow weary,
they will walk
and not be faint."
Isaiah 40:31

One of my favorite parts of my week
is to share God sightings with our
youth Sunday school class.
The kids love to share rainbows,
animals, and the adults often share
about birds.
This verse was my 2024 verse of the
year, I will not grow weary even
in the struggles that come.
Every time I see a large bird,
I take a moment to smile and
thank God for reminding me that
He is always with me; and I give thanks.

DEVOTIONAL CHECK -IN

DATE: _________________________   S M T W T F S

TODAY I'M GRATEFUL FOR

-
-
-

TODAY'S AFFIRMATION

- _______________________
- _______________________
- _______________________
- _______________________

SOMETHING I'M PROUD OF

- _______________________
- _______________________
- _______________________
- _______________________

NOTES / REMINDERS

17 | Finding comfort

"Do not fear, for I am with
you; do not be dismayed,
for I am your God.
I will strengthen you and
help you; I will uphold you
with My righteous
right hand."
Isaiah 41:10

Fear keeps us focused on the past or worried about the future. The Bible reminds us 365 times not to fear. We worry about our kid's future, the state of the world, and a laundry list of other things. In "A Charlie Brown Christmas," Linus says, "Fear not" as he is describing the birth of Christ. In this moment, he drops his beloved blanket because even he knows that in his fear where he needed a security blanket, that his God is bigger and has it.

DEVOTIONAL CHECK -IN

DATE: ________________________   S   M   T   W   T   F   S

TODAY I'M GRATEFUL FOR

-
-
-

TODAY'S AFFIRMATION

- ___________________
- ___________________
- ___________________
- ___________________

SOMETHING I'M PROUD OF

- ___________________
- ___________________
- ___________________
- ___________________

NOTES / REMINDERS

"I know the Lord is always with me. I will not be shaken, for He is right beside me."
Psalm 16:8

O Heavenly Father, in whom we live and
move and have our being,
we humbly pray you so to guide and
govern us by your Holy Spirit,
That in all the cares and occupations
of our daily life we may never forget you,
but remember that we are ever
walking in your sight.
For your name's sake.

Fifth century prayerbook

FREE THOUGHTS

DEVOTIONAL CHECK -IN

DATE: _______________________________   S M T W T F S

TODAY I'M GRATEFUL FOR

-
-
-

TODAY'S AFFIRMATION

- _______________________
- _______________________
- _______________________
- _______________________

SOMETHING I'M PROUD OF

- _______________________
- _______________________
- _______________________
- _______________________

NOTES / REMINDERS

"The Lord Himself goes before you and will be with you; He will never leave you nor forsake you. Do not be afraid; do not be discouraged."
Deuteronomy 31:8-9

Dear Heavenly Father,
Thank you for everything you do.
Please go before me and help me
get through every mountain,
I'm going to face today.
Please be near when it feels
too hard, and when I feel
like the world is crashing in.
In Jesus' Name.
Amen.

FREE THOUGHTS

DEVOTIONAL CHECK -IN

DATE: _______________________________   S   M   T   W   T   F   S

TODAY I'M GRATEFUL FOR

-
-
-

TODAY'S AFFIRMATION

-
-
-
-

SOMETHING I'M PROUD OF

-
-
-
-

NOTES / REMINDERS

"Peace I leave with you;
my peace I give you.
I do not give to you as the
world gives.
Do not let your hearts be
troubled and
do not be afraid."
John 14:27

Show us, good Lord,
The peace we should seek
The peace we must give
The peace we can keep
The peace we must forgo,
And the peace you have given in
Jesus our Lord.
-Contemporary Prayers for Public Worship

Give me strength and courage, Lord to
follow your chosen path for me without
fear, and without question.
You are the light of the world!

FREE THOUGHTS

DEVOTIONAL CHECK -IN

DATE: _______________________________   S   M   T   W   T   F   S

TODAY I'M GRATEFUL FOR

-
-
-

TODAY'S AFFIRMATION

- ___________________________
- ___________________________
- ___________________________
- ___________________________

SOMETHING I'M PROUD OF

- ___________________________
- ___________________________
- ___________________________
- ___________________________

NOTES / REMINDERS

"Splendor and majesty are before Him; strength and joy are in His place."
1 Chronicles 16:27

You can find joy not because of your
circumstances, but true joy
is in your faith and
knowing your purpose.

What do you think is your
purpose today?
Where do you find your joy?

DEVOTIONAL CHECK -IN

DATE: _______________________   S M T W T F S

TODAY I'M GRATEFUL FOR

-
-
-

TODAY'S AFFIRMATION

-
-
-
-

SOMETHING I'M PROUD OF

-
-
-
-

NOTES / REMINDERS

"The peace of God, which surpasses all comprehension, will guard your hearts and your minds in Christ Jesus."
Philipians 4:7

When you open the windows in the
morning, you don't have to beg the
fresh air to come in.
Instead it eagerly rushes in to greet you.
When you part the curtains in the
morning, the sun shines eagerly into your
room. The Bible tells us God's peace
is just like this,
It will flow into our hearts, if we let it.
Are you worried? Troubled? Anxious?
Don't try to navigate it alone.
Let God's peace flow in — like the
sunshine filling a dark room.

DEVOTIONAL CHECK -IN

DATE: _______________________   S M T W T F S

TODAY I'M GRATEFUL FOR

-
-
-

TODAY'S AFFIRMATION

- _______________________
- _______________________
- _______________________
- _______________________

SOMETHING I'M PROUD OF

- _______________________
- _______________________
- _______________________
- _______________________

NOTES / REMINDERS

"I lift my eyes to the hills.
From where does my
help come?My help comes
from the Lord, who made
heaven
and earth."
Psalm 121: 1-2

We can't do it alone. It feels like
we should be able to, but we can't.
On our hardest days, when
caffeine isn't covering it,
we need God.
We need Him to help us through the
sleepless nights
that have turned into days we can't
get through fast enough.
It's nice to remember
that God is our help.

DEVOTIONAL CHECK -IN

DATE: _______________________________   S   M   T   W   T   F   S

TODAY I'M GRATEFUL FOR

-
-
-

TODAY'S AFFIRMATION

-
-
-
-

SOMETHING I'M PROUD OF

-
-
-
-

NOTES / REMINDERS

"I will remain confident of this: I will see the goodness of the Lord in the land of the living. Wait for the Lord; be strong and take heart and wait for the Lord."

Psalm 27: 13-14

Believing there is good in the world,
helps us to see the good.
Moving along in your journey to find
peace with change, helps us see
opportunities for joy in our everyday
life.
Praying for ways to see opportunity
for inclusion, community connections,
ways to celebrate your faith; helps us
see the possibilities for a better future
for our families and our children.
Trusting that people really are good,
helps us learn there is hope for a
better tomorrow.

FREE THOUGHTS

DEVOTIONAL CHECK -IN

DATE: ______________________________   S   M   T   W   T   F   S

TODAY I'M GRATEFUL FOR

-
-
-

TODAY'S AFFIRMATION

-
-
-
-

SOMETHING I'M PROUD OF

-
-
-
-

NOTES / REMINDERS

25 Finding comfort

"I smiled on them when they had no confidence, and the light of my face they did not cast down."
Job 29:24

Dear Mama,

Remember today that God sees you, He sees all that you are doing to care for another. He sees the love that you pour into them every single day. He wants us to know that we are never alone, and that we are doing selfless work.

Close your eyes, lift your face to the light today and take a moment to enjoy the warmth of that pause.

Never alone, mama. Never alone.

DEVOTIONAL CHECK -IN

DATE: _______________________________   S   M   T   W   T   F   S

TODAY I'M GRATEFUL FOR

-
-
-

TODAY'S AFFIRMATION

-
-
-
-

SOMETHING I'M PROUD OF

-
-
-
-

NOTES / REMINDERS

"Not only that, but we rejoice in our sufferings, knowing that suffering produces endurance, and endurance produces character, and character produces hope, and hope does not put us to shame, because God's love has been poured into our hearts through the Holy Spirit who has been given to us."

Romans 5:3-5

As caregivers, we know the feeling of
enduring hard, lonely days.
The kind of days that feel like years.
God has promised us that the struggle
will not be in vain and that we will
always have hope.
Hope is the first and last thing that we
should hold onto.

What are some of your current hopes?

____
____
____
____

DEVOTIONAL CHECK -IN

DATE: ________________________________   S   M   T   W   T   F   S

TODAY I'M GRATEFUL FOR

-
-
-

TODAY'S AFFIRMATION

-
-
-
-

SOMETHING I'M PROUD OF

-
-
-
-

NOTES / REMINDERS

Love Conquers All

I always said that I wasn't sure I wanted to be a mom until the pregnancy test said pregnant. Then something switched and I knew that I needed to make myself a better person because it wasn't about me anymore. We endured a lot while you were in utero with the same consensus being that you were a miracle. You came into this world early. If we're being honest, I wasn't prepared. I was ordering things from Target while I was in labor with you.

When you arrived, you were whisked away to another hospital, and I was left with one picture of you to help me pump liquid gold to help you. It was you and me against the world those first couple of weeks, sweet boy. You became our happiness wrapped up in a little blanket. Everything you did was pure magic. We noticed that you loved life but were a man of few words. We didn't worry because you were born early. We were told you would catch up. When you didn't, we began our intervention journey.

I felt I had somehow failed you. What I thought would be just early intervention turned into our Autism/Apraxia journey. I don't regret anything about you for one second, sweet boy. You are the strongest human I know. You are the reason that I have everything in my adult life. Truth is, I'd be lost without you. I'm insanely proud of you. You have overcome so much in your ten years of life.

You, sweet Whitman, have a laugh funnier than the punchline,
you are smarter than all of us, and you are loved by so many.
Anyone who has ever been in your presence knows that they
have met someone special.
I like to think you brought a piece of heaven to us when we
needed it.

You have friends seek you out when you're outside to play or
invite you on playdates. I know in the beginning of your
diagnosis journey, I was scared and a little crazy. I wanted you
to be your best self. The world can be cruel and judgy. I wanted
to know you were on the right track. I've gotten over that
hump and I have realized that all that matters is that you're
happy. Your happiness is all that matters. I love that you walk
to the beat of your own drum with no apologies. I love that you
reset or disable any piece of technology. I still have no clue
what you did to our TV and why it's in Dutch. I love that you
giggle at chaos while it's happening. You prefer to jump in and
make it more chaotic. It shows just how brave you are. You are
the bravest human, Whitman. You came into this world when
you weren't ready and you haven't been stopped since.

 I'm so grateful for you and everything that you're doing. You,
my dear Whit, are going to change the world. And I cannot wait
to be in the front row cheering on. Or in the back row hiding
like you prefer. Either way, I'll be there. You are absolute
magic Whitman. Everyday with you is my favorite day.

You truly are one of the most extraordinary people I have ever known. Your gifts to this world are making a difference in ways you may not yet see. You have an incredible talent for making people smile, you can make anyone fall in love with you, just by being yourself. You acknowledge every person you see, you are always the first to say hello, and treat everyone you meet exactly the same. What a gift to watch you, and learn from your example of the purest forms of kindness for others.

You will never know how much you've changed my life, Jackson Bear. You've made me a better teacher. A better mother. Our family is who we are because you've shown us what love, patience, and inclusion means. I want you to know love in this home is never conditional, there is nothing that will ever change how fiercely we love, advocate, or search for more - for all of us.

It is important that you know that the moment you were placed into my arms, I knew we were in for an adventure. I never anticipated an extreme love for trains, mountains of DVDs, a room dedicated to model railroading, or any of your unique interests but I am so grateful that you share each one with me. Learning to navigate teaching skills through therapy, finding the best school, praying we were doing the best we could when resources were limited, and never giving up were all out of love and commitment to helping you succeed, my sweet boy. Thank you for being patient with me as I fumbled my way through. Thank you for forgiving me, loving me through, and for granting me grace as we walk through this journey together.

Your smile reminds me every single day that we have more to explore, more to uncover, more adventure! Every single day I know that I was meant to be your mama, sweet boy. Together we will climb this mountain, and bask in the sunshine that's waiting for us at the top.

You are a gift Jacks, and our family is so incredibly proud of you.

Thank you for teaching us all about the power of kindness, the gift of a friend, and the incredible gift of taking time to notice every small detail and how to create celebrations in the moments of each day.

I love you sweet boy, to the moon and back,and all the way down the railroad tracks.

"May you be strengthened with all power according to His glorious might so that you may have great endurance and patience."
Colossians 1:11

Every single week during my silent
prayers and moments of reflection,
I always ask God for more patience.
More patience with myself, my plans,
results of the work I'm doing.
What I think I always forget is...
God hears every prayer
but I am always in a hurry to receive an
answer. God has a sense of humor that
way, His time isn't always immediate...
funny how he's giving me exactly
what I'm asking him for without
even realizing my prayers are being
answered. Learn to love the wait...

DEVOTIONAL CHECK -IN

DATE: _________________________________   S   M   T   W   T   F   S

TODAY I'M GRATEFUL FOR

-
-
-

TODAY'S AFFIRMATION

-
-
-
-

SOMETHING I'M PROUD OF

-
-
-
-

NOTES / REMINDERS

"So also you have sorrow
now, but I will see you again,
and your hearts will rejoice,
and no one will take your
joy from you."
John 16:22

There's joy in the morning.
Growing up, I used to love
singing, "Trading My Sorrows."
My favorite line was
"Though the sorrow
may last for the night, the joy
comes in the morning."
I may sing it to myself on the days
when being a caretaker seems
like too much. There will be
joy and rejoicing soon.

DEVOTIONAL CHECK -IN

DATE: _______________________   S   M   T   W   T   F   S

TODAY I'M GRATEFUL FOR

-
-
-

TODAY'S AFFIRMATION

-
-
-
-

SOMETHING I'M PROUD OF

-
-
-
-

NOTES / REMINDERS

29 Love conquers all

"God blesses those who are humble, for they will inherit the whole earth.
God blesses those who hunger and thirst for justice, for they will be satisfied.
God blesses those who are merciful, for they will be shown mercy."
Matthew 5:5-7

Whatever you're going through today, I'd
like to pray for you. I pray His strength and
bravery wash over you, to help you feel
prepared for whatever troubles you
are facing.
Find strength in Him, find peace in Him.
Try to set down your anticipation for what
will come next, or the worry you are
carrying like over-stuffed suitcases.
Lean into your walk with the Lord,
find comfort there today knowing
He will never leave you,
He will not forsake you,
and He is always listening, friend.

DEVOTIONAL CHECK -IN

DATE: _________________________   S M T W T F S

TODAY I'M GRATEFUL FOR

-
-
-

TODAY'S AFFIRMATION

- _______________________
- _______________________
- _______________________
- _______________________

SOMETHING I'M PROUD OF

- _______________________
- _______________________
- _______________________
- _______________________

NOTES / REMINDERS

"Let your unfailing love be with us, Lord, even as we put our hope in you."
Psalm 33:22

Dear Lord,

Please help me remember
that your love is unfailing in my hardest
moments. Please remind me
that with my hope in you,
I'm unstoppable.

Amen.

DEVOTIONAL CHECK -IN

DATE: _________________________   S M T W T F S

TODAY I'M GRATEFUL FOR

-
-
-

TODAY'S AFFIRMATION   **SOMETHING I'M PROUD OF**

- _______________________   - _______________________
- _______________________   - _______________________
- _______________________   - _______________________
- _______________________   - _______________________

NOTES / REMINDERS

"And now these three remain: faith, hope, and love. But the greatest of these is love."
1 Corinthians 13:13

I often talk about love and the autism
diagnosis of my son together.
I asked in the early years, "why can't my
love for him be enough to take away his
struggles, God?" Over and over, I would ask
this out loud, expecting a response.
What I've learned as time has gone on,
it's God's love for me that gives me the
strength to give my son exactly what he
needs from me, and that my love for my
son, Jackson, that has allowed me to be
the person he needs.
The one to show him patience, to listen even
when he doesn't have the words, and to help
him explore the world,
so the world knows him.

DEVOTIONAL CHECK -IN

DATE: _______________________   S   M   T   W   T   F   S

TODAY I'M GRATEFUL FOR

-
-
-

TODAY'S AFFIRMATION

-
-
-
-

SOMETHING I'M PROUD OF

-
-
-
-

NOTES / REMINDERS

"Therefore we do not lose heart. Though outwardly we are wasting away, yet inwardly we are being renewed day by day. For our light and momentary troubles are achieving for us an eternal glory that far outweighs them all. So we fix our eyes not on what is seen, but on what is unseen, since what is seen is temporary, but what is unseen is eternal."
2 Corinthians 4:16-18

Dear Lord Jesus,

Thank you for this beautiful day. Please keep
me renewed when the world is crashing down
around me. Help me to be strong in the hard
moments of disability caretaking.
Remind me in the overwhelm that this
life, no matter how long, is only temporary,
and the best is yet to come when I'm
in eternity with you.
In your name.

Amen.

DEVOTIONAL CHECK -IN

DATE: _________________________   S M T W T F S

TODAY I'M GRATEFUL FOR

-
-
-

TODAY'S AFFIRMATION

-
-
-
-

SOMETHING I'M PROUD OF

-
-
-
-

NOTES / REMINDERS

"Your heart will be where your treasure is."
Matthew 6:21

I hope that you spend time today
closing your eyes and savoring a moment
that you never want to forget.
Hold close the things that make you smile,
the things that make you place your hand
over your heart because you want to hold
them there forever.
Those are our greatest gifts in life,
our treasures. The belly laughs of our
children, milestones, experiences that
take our breath away.
Close your eyes in those moments so that
you never forget them.
Take the time today to write them down.

DEVOTIONAL CHECK -IN

DATE: _______________________________   S   M   T   W   T   F   S

TODAY I'M GRATEFUL FOR

-
-
-

TODAY'S AFFIRMATION

- _______________________
- _______________________
- _______________________
- _______________________

SOMETHING I'M PROUD OF

- _______________________
- _______________________
- _______________________
- _______________________

NOTES / REMINDERS

"She dresses herself with strength and makes her arms strong."
Proverbs 31:17

This verse is a great reminder that we are
stronger when we put our strength in God.
I know that on sleepless nights, I forget to put
my strength in God and become very bitter
about the life I am privileged to have.
It isn't how I expected it, but I'm grateful that I
have it, and I'm grateful for a God
who carries me through.

How are you dressing yourself in strength?

____

____

____

____

DEVOTIONAL CHECK -IN

DATE: ________________________________   S   M   T   W   T   F   S

TODAY I'M GRATEFUL FOR

-
-
-

TODAY'S AFFIRMATION

-
-
-
-

SOMETHING I'M PROUD OF

-
-
-
-

NOTES / REMINDERS

"May the Lord make your love increase and overflow for each other and for everyone else, just as ours does for you."
1 Thessalonians 3:12

I have always loved and admired
Fred Rogers. He always said his ministry
was teaching children how to
love one another.
One of my favorite practices I've learned
from him is so simple, but yet so
powerful to practice in the quiet
moments of your day.
"Take a minute, close your eyes, and
think of all the people who have
loved you into the person you are today.
Some may be with you, some may be
far away, some may even be in heaven.
How honored they are to know you are
thinking of them in this moment."

____

____

____

____

DEVOTIONAL CHECK -IN

DATE: _______________________________   S M T W T F S

TODAY I'M GRATEFUL FOR

-
-
-

TODAY'S AFFIRMATION

-
-
-
-

SOMETHING I'M PROUD OF

-
-
-
-

NOTES / REMINDERS

"And let us consider how we may spur one another on toward love and good deeds."

Hebrews 10: 24-25

We all need a little bit of encouragement.
Knowing that we've been seen and heard
helps us, even on our hardest days. If
someone feels encouraged, they
usually try to encourage someone else.

How can you be encouraged?

Who can you encourage?

DEVOTIONAL CHECK -IN

DATE: ____   S   M   T   W   T   F   S

TODAY I'M GRATEFUL FOR

-
-
-

TODAY'S AFFIRMATION

- _______________________
- _______________________
- _______________________
- _______________________

SOMETHING I'M PROUD OF

- _______________________
- _______________________
- _______________________
- _______________________

NOTES / REMINDERS

"We have this hope as an
anchor for the soul,
firm and secure."

Hebrews 6:19

Every school year there is a verse of the
year at the kids' school.
"Hope is an anchor for the soul" was the
chosen verse for the '23-24 year.
Hope is such a powerful word, especially
when used within the school setting, I think.
We pray so much for the safety of our
children, that they will be accepted for
exactly who they are by their peers,
that they will be included, and most of
all that they will feel loved by the adults
who they are spending so much of their
time away from us with.
Hope that they feel loved is always
my prayer.

DEVOTIONAL CHECK -IN

DATE: _________________________   S   M   T   W   T   F   S

TODAY I'M GRATEFUL FOR

-
-
-

TODAY'S AFFIRMATION

- __________________
- __________________
- __________________
- __________________

SOMETHING I'M PROUD OF

- __________________
- __________________
- __________________
- __________________

NOTES / REMINDERS

"Rejoice always, pray
without ceasing, give thanks
in all circumstances; for this
is the will of
God in Christ Jesus
for you."
1 Thessalonians 5: 16-18

When we were in the NICU with our son
Whitman, the first few days were spent
listening to everything that
could happen. It was hard to process
everything. In those early days,
my husband and I decided to find
one thing we were grateful
for and one that made us happy.
Some days, we would be grateful that we
survived and our bed had clean sheets.
Nothing profound. 1 Thes. 5:16-18
became our verse to remind us and help us
find the good in our circumstances. What is
something you are grateful for? Something
that makes you happy?

FREE THOUGHTS

____

____

____

____

DEVOTIONAL CHECK -IN

DATE: _________________________________   S   M   T   W   T   F   S

TODAY I'M GRATEFUL FOR

-
-
-

TODAY'S AFFIRMATION

-
-
-
-

SOMETHING I'M PROUD OF

-
-
-
-

NOTES / REMINDERS

"The second is this, You will love your neighbor as yourself. No other commandment is greater than these." Mark 12:31

The Bible calls us to love our neighbor as ourself. Loving our neighbor is easy, we've been practicing the "golden rule" since we were in elementary school. But have you been practicing self love? God made us each in his own image. He looked at the world and thought that the world needed you in this world. How incredible is that? We need to do better in practicing self love. I know that the mom guilt is heavy, but we have to love ourselves in order to love our neighbor.

How can you love yourself better?

DEVOTIONAL CHECK -IN

DATE: _______________________________   S   M   T   W   T   F   S

TODAY I'M GRATEFUL FOR

-
-
-

TODAY'S AFFIRMATION

- ______________________________
- ______________________________
- ______________________________
- ______________________________

SOMETHING I'M PROUD OF

- ______________________________
- ______________________________
- ______________________________
- ______________________________

NOTES / REMINDERS

There's Always Hope

dear mama,

I know that you are tired and you're scared. Parenting can be heavy. Every decision can feel like it's life or death. I can remember researching everything to make sure that I was making the right decision on what kind of pouches to buy after Whitman was diagnosed. I began to question if I could do this and be his mother. You were meant to be this sweet child's mom. You know what they need when the world doesn't understand it. You know how to make them smile and what blanket goes with what mood. You get that the lined-up treasures are a communication method, not just a mess. You're the one who is up at 2:30 in the morning and manages to do everything on your list. You're a strong superhero in my eyes.

 In the early days, I was trying to balance a three-week-old and was ultimately convinced that I had ruined everyone's life by having her. I pumped during diagnosis appointments and tried not to lose it in the therapy center waiting room. It took an OT telling me that younger siblings are the answered prayer that any kiddo on her service needs. They help. I thought she was saying that to make me feel better, but she was right. Vivi helped Whit more in all aspects of his life as she got older. While some days, their never-ending fighting can drive me crazy, I never take it for granted because it's something siblings are supposed to do.

Know that this to shall pass. On a podcast I was listening to recently, the discussion of what you wish you could tell your younger self and someone said, "I wish I could tell my younger self that 'this too shall pass.' When you're in your lowest low, 'this too shall pass.' When you're in the highest highs, enjoy it because 'this too shall pass.'" Life has a way of giving you the highest peaks and the lowest valleys. But they all pass.

 As you get ready for the day or get ready to go to bed, I encourage you, sweet mama, to give it to God. Let Him handle your fears and worries. I know that you want to be in control when your world feels out of control, but let God help you navigate. This life wasn't meant to be done alone. My prayer is that you find a tribe that gets what you are going through and that God reminds you every day that he is here and that you and him can handle anything that life throws at you together. Just remember this too shall pass. It might hurt like a kidney stone but this too shall pass. Just remember, my dear, sweet Mama, are stronger than you will ever know, and you are the absolute best mom and so much more.

V,
lindsey

dear mama,

This season won't last forever.
One day parts of this journey will get easier and you'll look back and wonder how you did it, question how you made it through. I don't mean special needs parenting will get easier, but eventually you find a groove, or maybe you find help along the way.

You won't always be this sleep-deprived, exhausted, and worn down.
One day there won't be so many therapies, activities, projects happening that prevent you from getting your workout, or a nap in. Some day you'll have time to meet a friend for lunch again. You'll have time to get dressed and put lipstick on before you go.

Eventually there won't be staff shortages that seem to continually throw you and your child's routine completely for a loop. One day you won't have to work through hours of manic laughter, aggression, or meltdowns with no moment for yourself.

I know because we've been there, and then we came back, and I know there will be another side again.

Take my hand, lean in close, and listen ... you will make it through this, and you will show strength and grit that you never knew was in you. You will fight, and you will fail, but you will learn a love that can only be felt and not explained. Your heart will burst with pride when success comes your way, and it will shatter you into one million pieces when you see your child being excluded.

This journey of parenting a child with autism is unpredictable, it's exhausting, it often feels like an emotional roller coaster ride with no end... Just loops. There are moments where you find peace. You get a rare moment to breathe. And things don't feel quite so hard for a while.
And then one day the roller coaster starts again and you're back in the trenches.

But because we've been on all sides along the way, I can tell you that wherever you are right now... That's just a season. Our kids are always changing, growing, and so are we.

Hang on tight mama, and remind yourself, this is only a stage right now. This isn't the way it will be forever. And on the hardest days of all, lean in, ask God for strength, and wait for the whisper.

♡,
amanda

"Therefore do no worry about tomorrow, for tomorrow will worry about itself. Each day has enough trouble of its own. "
Matthew 6:34

Dear Lord,
Please help me to release control to you. For you know the great plans you have for me. I am laying down my anticipation for tomorrow's trouble at your feet. I need you today, tomorrow, and always. You are my strength, today I will do my best to stay in the moment, to see what you want me to see for this day!
Amen.

____

____

____

____

DEVOTIONAL CHECK -IN

DATE: _______________________   S   M   T   W   T   F   S

TODAY I'M GRATEFUL FOR

-
-
-

TODAY'S AFFIRMATION

-
-
-
-

SOMETHING I'M PROUD OF

-
-
-
-

NOTES / REMINDERS

"And we know that in all things God works for the good of those who love him, who have been called according to his purpose."
Romans 8:28

We have to hold onto God.
It can be hard sometimes when we are
in the thick of a hard season.
But God is working for the good of us.
We may not understand it, and it may be
hard to comprehend God's end game,
but we must trust Him through our
tears and hardest days.

DEVOTIONAL CHECK -IN

DATE: _______________________   S   M   T   W   T   F   S

TODAY I'M GRATEFUL FOR

-
-
-

TODAY'S AFFIRMATION

- _______________________
- _______________________
- _______________________
- _______________________

SOMETHING I'M PROUD OF

- _______________________
- _______________________
- _______________________
- _______________________

NOTES / REMINDERS

"You are my hiding place
and my shield; I hope in
Your word."
Psalm 119:114

My favorite discussion to have with youth is how do we pray? And why do we pray? I think we often think there is a right, or a wrong way to do something so it holds us back from just speaking what is on our heart. God wants to be our best friend, our refuge, our protector, so the best way to let God know us; is to talk to Him. Tell God about your worries, our fears, and even the good things that have happened to us. God wants us to grow our relationship with Him, and our reward for doing that? He provides us so much hope, and a place to escape the noise that distracts us in our day-to-day world.

DEVOTIONAL CHECK -IN

DATE: _______________________________   S   M   T   W   T   F   S

TODAY I'M GRATEFUL FOR

-
-
-

TODAY'S AFFIRMATION

-
-
-
-

SOMETHING I'M PROUD OF

-
-
-
-

NOTES / REMINDERS

"Blessed are the pure in heart, for they will see God."
Matthew 5:8

Dear Loving Heavenly Father,
Please help me to keep a pure heart,
even in my toughest moments today.
Help me navigate this day, and see you
in the process.
Please be near.

In Jesus' name.

Amen.

DEVOTIONAL CHECK -IN

DATE: _______________________________   S M T W T F S

TODAY I'M GRATEFUL FOR

-
-
-

TODAY'S AFFIRMATION

-
-
-
-

SOMETHING I'M PROUD OF

-
-
-
-

NOTES / REMINDERS

"And now, O Lord, for what
do I wait?
My hope is in you."
Psalm 39:7

You promise to go before me and
behind me, Lord.
I'm counting on You.
Stay right here with me.
I trust in you.
I will follow your lead.
I will walk with you,
faithfully.

DEVOTIONAL CHECK -IN

DATE: _______________________________   S   M   T   W   T   F   S

TODAY I'M GRATEFUL FOR

-
-
-

TODAY'S AFFIRMATION

-
-
-
-

SOMETHING I'M PROUD OF

-
-
-
-

NOTES / REMINDERS

"For God alone, O my soul,
waits in silence. for my hope
is from Him. He alone is my
rock and my salvation,
my fortress;
I shall not be shaken."
Psalm 62:5-6

The wise man built his house
on the rock, so when the rain came, the
house stood firm. God is the rock
on which we need to build
our faith to stand firm in our belief
in any season.
Recording Artist Chris Tomlin sings,
"If our God is for us, then who
can ever stop us?"
Having a firm foundation
in Him can help you be unstoppable.

FREE THOUGHTS

DEVOTIONAL CHECK -IN

DATE: _________________________________   S M T W T F S

TODAY I'M GRATEFUL FOR

-
-
-

TODAY'S AFFIRMATION

-
-
-
-

SOMETHING I'M PROUD OF

-
-
-
-

NOTES / REMINDERS

"You are the light of the
world... Let your light shine
before men, that they may
see your good works and
glorify you
Father in heaven."
Matthew 5:14

I often think about how autism has
brought some of the brightest parts
of our story into my life.
The people it's connected me with,
the lessons I've learned, the love
that has grown out of it.
And I often think it's because my son
is never afraid to show the world
exactly who he is.
Shiny parts, noisy parts, curious
questions we would shy away from
asking; He is a bright light in this
sometimes dark world.
He shines his light to glorify the Lord.

DEVOTIONAL CHECK -IN

DATE: _______________________________   S M T W T F S

TODAY I'M GRATEFUL FOR

-
-
-

TODAY'S AFFIRMATION

-
-
-
-

SOMETHING I'M PROUD OF

-
-
-
-

NOTES / REMINDERS

"The do not fear bad news;
they confidently trust the
Lord to care for them. They
are confident and fearless
and can face their foes
triumphantly."
Psalm 112: 7-8

Dear Loving God,
Thank you for another day on this Earth.
Please help me to walk by faith and not
by sight, knowing that you
have my best interest at heart.

In Jesus' name.

Amen.

____

____

____

____

DEVOTIONAL CHECK -IN

DATE: ___________________________   S   M   T   W   T   F   S

TODAY I'M GRATEFUL FOR

-
-
-

TODAY'S AFFIRMATION

-
-
-
-

SOMETHING I'M PROUD OF

-
-
-
-

NOTES / REMINDERS

"Casting all your anxieties
on him, because
he cares for you."
1 Peter 5:7

God, please prepare me for all of my
worries and troubles that I will
face today.
I know that I can do anything as long
as you are the one making me strong.
I am reminded that I never have to
face these fears alone.

Amen.

DEVOTIONAL CHECK -IN

DATE: _______________________________   S   M   T   W   T   F   S

TODAY I'M GRATEFUL FOR

-
-
-

TODAY'S AFFIRMATION

- _______________________________
- _______________________________
- _______________________________
- _______________________________

SOMETHING I'M PROUD OF

- _______________________________
- _______________________________
- _______________________________
- _______________________________

NOTES / REMINDERS

"Rejoice in hope, be patient
in tribulation,
be constant in prayer."
Romans 12:12

Dear Lord,
Please be with me when I face
tribulations and remind me of the prize
ahead. Please be with me
when my patience is wained.
Thank you for the hope that
I have in you.
Thank you for letting me have
this time to pray with you.
Amen.

DEVOTIONAL CHECK -IN

DATE: _______________________   S M T W T F S

TODAY I'M GRATEFUL FOR

-
-
-

TODAY'S AFFIRMATION

-
-
-
-

SOMETHING I'M PROUD OF

-
-
-
-

NOTES / REMINDERS

"I waited patiently for the Lord; He turned to me and heard my cry. He lifted me out of the slimy pit, out of the mud and mire; He set my feet on a rock and gave me a firm place to stand. He put a new song in my mouth, a hymn of praise to our God."

Psalm 40: 1-3

If you have been struggling with your faith and have been wanting to return to church, this is your invitation to try. If you've been wondering if God is listening, He is.
He knows the plans He has for us, we have to be patient and stay the course.
Some days these feel like impossible mountains to climb, but you can do anything, mama.
We simply just have to try.

DEVOTIONAL CHECK -IN

DATE: _______________________________   S   M   T   W   T   F   S

TODAY I'M GRATEFUL FOR

-
-
-

TODAY'S AFFIRMATION

- _______________________________
- _______________________________
- _______________________________
- _______________________________

SOMETHING I'M PROUD OF

- _______________________________
- _______________________________
- _______________________________
- _______________________________

NOTES / REMINDERS

"But this I call to mind, and therefore
I have hope: The steadfast love
of the Lord never ceases;
His mercies never come to an end;
they are new
every morning; great is your
faithfulness."
Lamentations 3:21-23

Every morning God renews our mercies; we just need to have faith. I love this verse because it reminds me of one of my favorite hymns. Music can be so healing. Lyrics can hit our soul in our happiest and hardest moments. I can hear a song and be taken back to some of my favorite memories. Songs can also make you feel God's presence when you hear them. They give you goosebumps and make you feel like you are in the presence of the kingdom.

What are some songs that make you feel the presence of God?

____

____

____

____

DEVOTIONAL CHECK -IN

DATE: _______________________   S   M   T   W   T   F   S

TODAY I'M GRATEFUL FOR

-
-
-

TODAY'S AFFIRMATION

- _______________________
- _______________________
- _______________________
- _______________________

SOMETHING I'M PROUD OF

- _______________________
- _______________________
- _______________________
- _______________________

NOTES / REMINDERS

"Truly, I tell you, if you have faith as small as a mustard seed, you can say to this mountain, 'Move from here to there,' and it will move. Nothing will be impossible for you."
Matthew 17:20

Dear Mama,
As you wrap up this devotional,
we want you to know you are not alone.
We are cheering, praying, and clapping for
you through whatever life throws at you.
You don't need the faith of massive religious
leaders. You need the faith of a mustard
seed. Our prayer for you is that you know
your worth. Being a caregiver can feel like a
thankless job most days, but God sees you;
He knows your worth and that you are a
beautiful jewel. Please hold onto the hope
that brighter days are on the horizon with
God writing your story.

DEVOTIONAL CHECK -IN

DATE: ________________________________   S M T W T F S

TODAY I'M GRATEFUL FOR

-
-
-

TODAY'S AFFIRMATION

-
-
-
-

SOMETHING I'M PROUD OF

-
-
-
-

NOTES / REMINDERS

"I pray that from His glorious, unlimited resources He will empower you with inner strength through His Spirit. Then Christ will make His home in your hearts as you trust Him. Your roots will grow down into God's love and keep you strong. And may you have the power to understand, as all God's people should, how wide, how long, how high, and how deep His love is.

Ephesians 3: 16-18